PAN'S DANCE

Pan's Dance

New and Selected Poems

REBECCA LAW

RESOURCE *Publications* · Eugene, Oregon

PAN'S DANCE
New and Selected Poems

The selected poems of this collection first appeared in Wild, An Anthology of Verse edited by Joan Fenney and published by Ginninderra Press; Mountain Secrets: An Anthology of Verse, edited by Joan Fenney and published by Ginninderra Press; and my own previous poetry collections including Lilies and Stars by Picaro Press, In My Days and In My Sleep by Interactive Publications, and Earthly Darling Came by Ginninderra Press.

Resource Publications
An Imprint of Wipf and Stock Publishers
199 W. 8th Ave., Suite 3
Eugene, OR 97401

www.wipfandstock.com

PAPERBACK ISBN: 978-1-7252-7857-8
HARDCOVER ISBN: 978-1-7252-7858-5
EBOOK ISBN: 978-1-7252-7859-2

Manufactured in the U.S.A.   08/12/20

I play Haydn after a dark day
and feel the simple warmth in my hands.
—Tomas Transtromer

Contents

A Holy Night—By Way of Explanation

The cartoonist thought is easy to be happy
and the patient asked why he was most often sad.

Morning rain saturated the canvas chairs
on the breakfast terrace; and a late sun
shone hard till they dried.

The new house creaked and snapped
with growing pains; and an old oak
groaned as it met once more with wind.

A willy wagtail turned east to west
in an eyeblick; yet the duck was forever
far from the pond.

Stars clustered, soared and arranged the
constellation of the Southern Cross
and our wild thunderstorm brought lightning.

The pillows on the bed were soft
and some hard, whilst day into night

was an upward movement—the ground
more dark than a newly expired match.

An Illustration for Nest Builders

Gabled roofs
so that
the hail breaks
to fall as particles,
flakes, the rain
with less momentum,
branches and smaller branches
with leaves to fall as
laymedowns,
so that
inside the last room
is least often
a kitchen for its roof:
the spine of an open book
the downstairs candle lights
empty pages with a centred
shadowline
so that
the night, for all its stars,
is in windows,
not ominous over our heads.

To a Sparrow

There's a line of thought
starting with a charcoal prayer,

a morning sun abiding,
the short and long of twigs,

my crowea exalata,
a presence of heart;

that shadowlike follows
in small bird feet,

even, dressed in finery,

doggedly pulling at my skirts,

the rubbed tear-ducts, to shade;

where almost stopped
you are listening
to small songs

your whole life,
a line of thought

you could question
as to the necessity of rain-breaks
overhead, in a hot month.

Kalorama Park

I.

mist,
when you leave be atomic
else not wake again;

if I were you
I would pursue,

raindrops closest to my own
for a chain-reaction-exit

like little kisses,

away with the winds,
mist.

II.

wide road
how often I say Wordsworth
when I see you

like a conception.

III.

cumulus
i can see blue skies
vast and wide

fill spaces
between
each of you

so weather
is incongruous

but generally
your stormy effects
dominate

and my shivering
is more reverence
than dislike, say–

Snapshot

For every green pine tree
a small, fresh clearing,
shades of air unkissed,
drawn in—the feet bare
imprinting on cool sand.

From heights, a seagull
noses depths past some
outermost wave only
to then soar upwards,
traverse a blue sky
with rapid wingbeats
& glide. The music soft
becomes loud becomes
soft in endless repetition.

At night, the glass lamp
is lit within, a balcony kept
by a screen carries breezes
from a darkening earth,
for every day, a turned stone.

Coming (II)

A man tries to say farewell
by walking in winter shoes
and clothes the downhill
of a beach embankment,
negotiating the moist, heavy
sand a fair portion of the
shoreline. His thirtyish
hands half in each of his
trousers side pockets, a gaze
that wants to look forward
but confessionally looks down
regularly: and this way speaks.

A journeyer climbs down
a mountain, the summit's
revelatory light and true, utmost perfection
held as if there were only one heart
one could love for a lifetime

And there appears to be
singing from females with high voices
as in a chant from another land

and home feels as vast as the whole of earth
but invariable in offering peace.

Pastoral

Charcoal artist
& sylvan field
(where crossed, quiet
Daphne): violets
grow, scenting with
heady perfumes
his century,
an impression
like the darkness
of afternoons
or dusk, early
night, romancing.

Data

Those star-shaped fragments
of blossom you brush
from our timber table
with both hands

like dust: we are sure
they are not. Though they fall
effortlessly and share the visible
colours of yellow and white.
Without them, we share our tea
on a summer afternoon
in a stranger's courtyard. I
scoop one soundlessly
from my porcelain cup
with a silver teaspoon
while you speak, resting it
on a saucer, saturated;
and see the paradox. Though
not seemingly a star I am
no longer sure it may not be.
In our conversation there is a
flame which burns with a
sharp red colour sparking at
times into atmosphere. And
though it burns it is too
ancient to be hot. What we

shared was immediacy, saw
the flowers which resemble
stars. And behind the brightness
the forms which are, shining.

New Work

Making a Tower Out of Packing Boxes

As I held my cup
of hot tea with both
hands, I looked into
its half-filled centre
to see the shadows
of my splayed fingers
showing through the
white porcelain;
and I thought of
that word 'here', as
being both
my hands and
the soft sunlight
between their
patterning, the
wind entering
via the open door
of the balcony,
the ocean falling.
At night, a moon
flat as a tablet
of stone and illumined
on the lower arc
to its left side,
letting the star
beneath it try

out its strength.
Then today,
sunlight so bright
it flooded the grasses
and the mountains
with entire warmth,
touching something
only to bounce off it
so quickly it left sparks
of jewel everywhere,
airborne as bliss;
a lone gull folding
down its wings.

After Election Night

Where was the euphoria
in the yards of broken streamers

bitumen streets of stillness

a young adult at the open
rear doors of his parked van
dodges the fall of an eco-friendly
coffee mug whilst dressing

Behind alps of heaping clouds
an atmosphere of sky that exudes
a dense deep blueness misty

alluring as sea cliff winds Did

they hide the maracas intended
to shake or the sharpened sticks

ready for brandishing tree trunks
with wonky, spirited heart motifs

the hazy dreams they took to
their lips in bars with eyes
troubled by numbers that scrolled

over like green figures in cash registers

someone in a crowd saying won't you
sing, won't you just sing And for hours

house lights switched on glowing

Now morning bleakness except
a musical lulling of text dings
on my phone that could be

cyber space already earthbound
aka mission succour happening

Journeys

Even six years since moving -
Sunday afternoons on a balcony
eating lunch—the seaplanes flying
overhead sound like lawnmowers
leaving the fresh scent of cut grass
in their trails, bright patches of
Spring sunlight catching the path,
cream brick walls with a warmth
reminiscent of summer days spent
swimming in neighbour's Clark
pools: stark, cobalt blue interiors.

Here, it's different, one more
weekend when you might have
taken the bike up and down the long
country driveway or wandered the garden
snapping off flowers for mother's
kitchen vase. If you're not home
on a bar stool reading emails, or
lying across your bed writing
entries to your diary, you are
at the beach, book in hand.

Except the light and shade
seems exquisitely perfect,
at times sparkling like new light

& others, soft and ebbing toward
the true meaning of grey, the less
severe, the intermediate between
life and death, angelic in its
weightlessness. A patterning
of leaves that flickers in wind
currents. Interstate, country to
seaside, the small improvements.

Term Holidays

Autumn weather has a way of seducing,
the mind sailing from cloud-grey atmospheres
of wait and emptiness, to gold across oceans
at sunrise, the seas outstandingly smooth,
atmospheres of light and breathiness. Yet,
when it comes to rain there is a frankness
that awakens all over again, not like eyes
blinking with sweet life into morning but now,
in afternoon, sharpening in gaze. Children
alone on the street, walk in pairs at a quickened
pace, bring out coins from their pockets and
verbalise hurried shopping lists—vegemite scrolls,
white toast, the walk becoming a run, heads
lowered to one another at random to swap coins,
recheck the list. At the sports club, a group of
teenage girls shriek with laughter as their friend
unpacks her bag exclaiming "oh my god,
I forgot my gym top." At my desk, the sky
darkens toward nightfall and the forecast, storm,
the yellow timber deepening in colour and the text
on my notebook starting to stand out from the blaze
of background. A silence that makes the sound
of my bedside clock louder than usual, the lamp above
the four-storey bookshelf, more radiant. The words
poetry and fire and the last word 'after'. How, after,
more than ever, he said, love is what mattered.

Final Months of a Ph.D.

The oak is starting to bloom
small flowers in pale yellow

and I start to doubt, one,
whether the clear sparsity of
its green leaves is for much
longer, and two, if the dead
parts of them, the colour of earth,
will soon be intercellular to
to the heavens. I see it's

largely due to the Currawong
who frequents, turns his back
to the window and snaps off a
twig mid-flight, his yellow eye
tilted in an upturned gaze.

And rain. I've also changed my
mind about the parking, how
when I first moved it seemed
the space was even smaller
than the last and the last

was smaller than the previous
space. So that, next time
I move it would be smaller
still and what would I do
then, with the car, giant:

now I'm not so worried. Even
when my birthday falls on a
Monday, all I do is make the
lunch break special. And since

the liturgist told me not to
say the response is but rather
just to say it outright, that also,
seemed quite good. Plus

Christmas. Already, the hushed
song practise of attributed stars.

Summer

A book discarded in the late hour of sleep
lies upturned on carpet beside my bed

where a moth finds it a worthy missal
for her own slumbering, the dust-heavy wings

resting familiarly amidst plot summaries,
biographies and recommendations

whilst on the far side of the room,
her lover treads cautiously downhill
of the pleated cotton valance. . .

It's Christmas, almost the New Year

so I take up the book with moth
and walk it shyly to her pair, stepping back
as I lower my find to ground level,

mild sleeper to valiant moth of the slopes.

To my astonishment the close encounter
awakens old fear and sudden flight as the pair

rebuke each other vehemently and fill
the air with sudden and glittering dust. . .

I could tell you about it, world, as the

cane chair rocks on the study patio
in wind and evokes memories of dad

- most likely angels, and the tall room

fills with the pattern of clouds
from an overcast sky, the sound of rain

just audible. . ..

Or the sand path fashioning pebbles
which ascends into blue skies,

the sharp taste of salt from a nearby ocean

and gracious salutations from flecked-brown or milk-white
butterflies traversing your passage as you jog on,

their silence so perfect it seems they speak words,
beautiful utterances of love, pleasures, thankfulness.

Or the darkness of night which seems mysterious
as moonlight catching a hillside of lawn

or a single star assigned a Sunday vigil.

Yet the trees rustle and the timber
pillars of the terrace creak and grey

in new light, my sister's muted conversation
with mother hums in another room

and the purple Armenia flowers
hemming the coastal walk sway memorably
from their tall slight stems

into tomorrow's pattern of daylight and movement
into your wildest but closest of all dreams.

Time Ahead

Post-sleep, today, everything was small.
Morning, at first, before it grew to a heat
that hit my back like a warm hand –
a favourite and also, strong,

then hanging cascades of thrip

which swarmed suspended in air
and stuck to my face, legs
and arms as I ran through
them unseeingly, wiping them off
frantically, desperate to breathe again,

noticing afterwards ants on sandy gravel—

the same, I thought, or very much like
as insect armies- Then twigs, snapped to

halves by autumnal dryness, crooked,
thin, strewn copiously across the bitumen

road; and shadows from their trees, faint,
dappled whilst vistas opened up streets

to azure, glossy river views, jetties
with painted white railings. Always
the sun growing warmer, stronger

& a tiny lizard strutting past me on
two hind legs, so perfectly miniscule
I not only jumped but gasped "Dinosaur!"
in disbelief. A wild shrub of forget-me-knots
in light purple, quick with scenting the breeze,

some white pebbles furnishing the curve of
the gnarly, bayside nature trail near home,

the singular door key I carried with a bright
yellow plastic tag, the mailbox unfulfilled,
the new text to a mobile phone left behind
desktop and that little term of endearment.

After Flight

Outside late with a small
hand torch lighting the path.

Across grass that takes
footprints as traces. Winter

will bury things, a wild
concoction of storm
elements. Air is the touch

of granite stones
with no flowerless moss, water-
less. My face rounded, the

rose brought forward, static
heat leaving tiny
pores. Near a hill's dark

summit, a view of evening
sky whose silver backdrop
holds in its front sphere a
large map of invented
continents. Across a distant

hillside, electric lights span
barred and golden or sharp,
dotted and living in twilight.

Square, small and bronze,
a lavishing of red flecks.

Above my gaze wind blows
the heavy shaded boughs
of trees so they make a
song out of the dance. Autumn

loses its longing in the
very moment. I, also,

downhill in my dark descent
chasing the cloud
of my torch, never too

far away and soaring
over the bitumen road.
A game, and a lost moon.

Othernesses

Winter's light hemming great clouds
with a tributary of brightness: stars
pre-flight, mid-drift then sundown,
shadows of birds with practised wings
outstretched, tilted in downward
dives of nightfall, silver calls into
cold air then a pink wash of hours: rose.
Candles and phone calls, those other rooms
imperceptible for the captivation of a loved one's
voice except the warmth of flames I watch
with the eyes of my mind elsewhere, some
place unknown but alluring for the mystery
even your double backed word goodnight
only decorates as it might a tree: field of lilac.

Small Music

For so long the constellation
of the Southern Cross
set right of my balcony
view, evenings looking up
and turning it in the mirrored
drawing of my hand
before indoor Grace. Now, only
a small yellow star for which
brightness comes easily. My sister,
interstate, grieving, is there,
somehow in the sweetness of its
strength: my mother saying that
when she falls, she falls
heavily and helplessly. But
now she is recovering like the
star is only just growing. I can
hear the ocean falling as I read
a catalogue of books after
dinner with it resting on my knees,
slowly circling the best looking
under lamplight, or perhaps, at that
late hour, the most magic of all.

The Couple by the Window

(Returning to Hiroshima: For Peter Dale Scott)

They sit side by side
on a low ledge beside
an unfurnished window,

the women's navy blue
spring smock patterned
by a small, traditional

print. Outside, the landscape

sweeps behind them, indistinctly.
A scene of pale skies and grey earth.

Even trees there, occasional,
refuse movement, are desolate.

The husband speaks of their
fear, of how, when the wind
blows, radiation levels rise

and he gestures to a small-
scaled monitor beside them,
pulsing with its latest results.

In the same village, flowers
in pink and red have bloomed
out of longstanding cherry trees.

The beginning starts from the end.

For the couple, to know what
is held in their loved ones eyes

is to sit this way, waiting for
the wind they hear passing,
to carry the past through.

Yet what grows there, side
by side. What has already, grown.

Monday, Sundown

Behind rows of low-level
vacated buildings, clouds queue
in soaring, northbound trajectories
across a sky of dusk that
bleeds rose pink into cold blue.

A streetlamp hovers over
a large oak, illumining its centre
junction so that canopies above
seem weighted in darkness, hold

the ghost of birdlife's profane legend
Larry, who flew continents to build
nest after nest and stole heart
after heart before losing his own

to some sort of madness that
stranded him and was ultimately
his downfall. In the supermarket

there's a village code for walking
among aisles with swiftness,
motivation and solitude. Across

backyard fences, down laneways
crickets sound out a muted drone
that could just as well be a recording
for its exquisite perfection and
muskiness. I phone mum again

from my kitchen like I'm phoning
batman, imagining the hospital
phone in her private room

flashing a square red light as it
rings—and when she answers
after only three, it's still
the same feeling: I got batman.

Correspondingly

I sat beside a guitar tonight,
as accident would have it,
and found myself staring at the instrument
– for it wasn't ordinary.

This is after last night
when you prompted:
if I could imagine a flock
of flamingos arriving
home to their lake.

So I did, and that night,
which comes after
the drawing you sent me,
of what you had made

(for the flamingos),

I heard nothing and saw
so much. It wasn't black
and white like your image
regrettably. I liked

your image being that way,
and for other reasons.

The guitar had songs
buried inside it that

obviously were studied
by angels, for you could
just tell without touching
it was light inside. Our

talk was like that,
about birds, home,
waiting. I thought
the next day I'd have

to look this topic up;
but not tonight. You'd
been swimming and I,
running the hills, valleys

of abiding love. Suffice
to say I see a lot of pink,
green and blue merging.
The hours of labour
drawing your black and white
sketch and my God,

that beautiful guitar.

Mechanics of a Flower Press

Walking home through the village
one Friday evening, the streets and lanes

seem unrecognisable. The entrance
courtyard of an Italian café festooned
with coloured lights. Couples dine

one across the table from the other,
their closeness proximal as well as
emanating—the same timber tale on

which a glass or piece of crockery is
scraped one side to the other, as
offerings. A sound which chimes from
one small table to the next. Ahead of me

a child boy walks his vanilla ice-cream
along the sidewalk, his soft marle trousers
carrying the repeated motif of a
dark grey dog, red sneakers walking
the shadow of his grandfather's own.

From a distant corner, a thin waiter
steps out a wine shop holding a
large white cardboard box of beer;

stops once; and moves on with a
clear destination. I am almost home

and can smell the rain on the lawns,
three days in which we rose in darkness
and returned home in darkness. Yet

early this morning there was a brightness
almost born of the night. Today's sky
only pale. The sun assuredly present

is a memory and today is a new image
which comes from the same city
yet has its place in plazas with fountains,
water that tastes of the silver and gold
coins that dapple its floor of stone.

What was is Cavafy said: "This city
will always pursue you"? I have forgotten
from where my raft left and the place
and time it arrived here. These twelve

hours have shown the music of
accomplishments, comfort from the
depths of a pitch blue night. Only to
beckon. We are awake. We are awake.

Intermezzo

There is destitution in the ocean,
like a boat at home in Autumn
seas. Light rain. On my face
and on my limbs, my running
through changes me. There is
joy in the newness. A yellow
globe lightens a whole room
and the oak's leaves hang,
glisten outside one window.
A venetian blind slats daylight
monochromatically. Without
the yellow globe, I would be
resting in shadows. The pages
of my book, instead coloured,
its inked black words pitched
in conversation, snug, hushed.

Paper, Rock, Scissors

Here, day has gone to night
and the moon stares out
like a cold stone wreathed
in stars half-made arc. No one

sings in the dark air, yet the glowing
offset of light and intermittent
blinking of stellar presencing
phrases a music not yet
put to sound. The door is

shut to home and from
a balcony's terrace, dark trees
absorb the blackly sky
like they are soldiers –
outside the child of their hearts.

The leaf blowers have guttered
Autumn but its woody perfume
moves through air as quixotic
incense, crisp with promised

rain. Quietly, sounds of distant
traffic flow like a gushing stream.
And home takes on a flatness
personifying boundlessness.

Cosmopolitan Sundays

From an open thesaurus
wafts a scented world
& speech hovers in
keywords: 'adequacy',
'essay' or pocket-sized
offshoots. 'Chaplet',
'honeyed', 'beastly'.

Outside, an aviary of
lorikeets sing practice
songs for more than an
hour before tiring to
silence. Light vaults

through venetians like
ecstatic stars; and across
the kitchen window, a grey
miner bird flies a swift
pathway upward. From a

world of rising dust, colours
subside to the beatific and
quiet. At the supermarket

near noon, a small, black
tethered puppy with

tight fur like velvet,
sits back on its hind legs
and extends the mood. His
mouth firmly closed without
a whimper, excepting the bottom
row of tiny, square, newly polished
white teeth which stay exposed,
buttressing the upper lip
and supervising the army with
a pointed fang either side. Although

I smile and stare, his dark eyes
observe me this way—unblinking
and statuesque. Time moves

the brass needles of a clock,

children walk streets track suited
and parents linger ahead with
beach hair. Even my ecstatically lit room

subdues then to the deeper hues
of closure. I can hear trucks

move off along the faraway
highway, piano music saying
things in notes: "first they go
there, then they leave there"
and smell a musky moon.

Elsewhere, Come Dusk

In that time, a crescent
moon hung over earth
facing stars some distance

North-East. Only a sky spoke
then, leaving us in a wintering
exhaustion of light: but for

this luminous tête-à-tête.

Wind blows around corners
as though for a first time,

someone forgot to close
the garden gate. Cricket song

hums so loudly you can
feel the air vibrate
with resonance. Whilst there

is a greater uncertainty
in the depth of a tree bough's
agitation. Sometimes, distant

traffic. Toward the back
of my apartment block

a sensor turns on a corner
light set diagonal
from the eaves; and a

black cat falls to its back
and writhes in a movement
of utter bliss. Across concrete

steps, the product of another

fall, a large piece of bark lies
strewn. I fancy it a future

receptacle of rust blossom;
and skip the step it owns.

Wild March

The sounds of distant traffic
can only be imagined and develops
sense through the luminous colours
they evoke, like a journey
through night: there are luminous
reds, greens and blues that ribbon
and merge, ribbon and separate.

A morning that never exactly
leaves an overcast sky, sounds of
breakfast crockery, made musical
by silver utensils no longer
audible but ghosted and present.

The large, black currawong with its yellow
eye, who palpably sat in the tree beside
the kitchen and oversaw lives
in silence before his call to fly
upwards; fanned his wings
and revealed their hidden whites.

Radio music speaks of a girl
on a journey of sorrow
who finds empowerment in
a single dress. The pine trees

I pass during travel appear uniform,
the filing, another sort of navigation.

Five pm, returning and the
crockery ghosts come alive
once more, the girl seeking her
dreams in a dress vanishes
from thought, a house starting
with an outdoor light
comes alive as a moon

to a lake. The laundry drying
out of the night air, drifts along
a shower rail from hangers,
the breeze behind it from
a high rectangular window frame
slid open, a panel of midnight tones
just short of stars. I hand it over,
late of dusk, to the currawong.

Of Speech

I am living in a day of full sunlight
and not asleep when birds
pass over in pursuit, one
after the other at only
a short distance: level.

Neither—dreaming when
in that sky toward which
my face is turned ,there
is only brightness. As though
it were a place different

from ours. Different in a way
I can only tell you is
like a sound instead of
a word or even, a complete

phrase. Except what it
speaks of is a language
I can barely understand,
it is so much like waking

from an evening of sleep,
from being both asleep
and involved in a dream

to having dawnlight come
and then state with simplicity
it is here : it is brightness,

it is morning. For which I
can only offer my own
darkness, some soft dream
through which your
intent appeared manifest.

Adagio for Day

The rain has stopped.

There is an ensemble
of coloured birds
singing only the melody
to a larger piece of music.

My waking feels timed.

Late morning, a single
evocation. The cloud is

slow to leave and drifts
imperceptibly. Across
shorelines, skies are tinged
with sharp, yellow light.

The whole expanse above
this shimmers away from

any sort of blueness.

A line of cars follows

the curve of a cliffside
journey, whilst a couple

astride a motorbike
meander the inside
verge; and that way,
remain absorbed. At

home, someone plays
the hour through in front
of an open piano, someone

else makes a pot of
Chinese tea and the tree

fulfilling the length of a
kitchen window, perfects stillness
even though its most stricken

parts, grey, barren and brittle

beg compassion. At my desk

progression is a slow dance
that steps the greater forward
than takes steps back. In the

black and white image of
a shooting star, for instance,
day captures night: just to hold.

One. Clover

It was only this morning
early, I watched a small
grey bird play at a white
thread of cotton strung
hammock style from lane
to lane of the clothes hoist

The way I would read
an anthology of love
poems, flitting front to back
to the insides to understand
what it generally was, what it
seemed and what it
was to me in my heart.

Then late tonight driving home
in the middle of winter,
the darkness always seeming
more black, more pitch, more
outside than I'd thought
experienced. A moon round,

and spherical with an underside
illumined so it shone upon
it's one, lowly, adjacent star

like a conversation about day –

familiar but especially enchanting
in the fact it could be regarded
as past and then alive in the tension

of love: meaning joys, eyes sore
from recalling sorrows, crying laughter.

Two. Star-flower

The young performer's piano
recital playing renditions
of Bach and Schumann
through and into the atmosphere
of darkness, late evening,
winter.

A dying star shoots
downwards at a diagonal
away from the buildings
lit internally with their domestic
warmth's, kitchen pendants, dining room
lamps, porch Christmas lights
flashing at intervals in differing colours.
in the star's wake, lavender shadows
like dust particles set against the depth
of night illumined—for thus . . ..

Only Tuesday, I cook risotto
with two pans and try to salvage
a document lost to cyberspace
that late afternoon after a library
computer shut off my session
unexpectedly, the hour of closure
arriving too soon. Earlier,
I was thinking about a friend

who mentioned a time he prayed
whilst it snowed on white jonquils
& I thought slowly of white on white
becoming ashen—understanding why.

Three. Rose

Half a moon cut through at the diagonal
by night, the lower left a sphere
of the most pure whiteness, the sort
which ebbs: a reflection in a pool
of atmospheric colours tinged by earth.
Latino music on tonight's radio
left me thinking of the flower rose
in scent, beauty and thorns –
the reason I was never a seamstress
and the grace of the fact.
I didn't mention it but besides the moon
there was also a bright star gazing upon it;
and the house under construction
beside my own yesterday, installed
a large rock where you might expect
the household mailbox—so again,
something beautiful to regard: as rose.

Four: Candle

For my friend whose facial tumour
won't diminish with haste,
"only a shadow of his love. . ."
for my two friends that I see
and cry with joy,
"only a shadow of his love"
for my friend whose greeting
instructs goodness,
"only a shadow of his love"
for my friend in whom loss
lessens with gain,
"only a shadow of his love"
for my friend in which day
is a journey toward gold,
"only a shadow of his love"
for my friend who is always first,
my mother: a birthday candle.
"only a shadow of his love. . ."

Five: Black

In the deepness, soft
light covers its flame
to hear breathing: in
wanting to sound out
my heart alone, silence
comes like a whispered
kiss. I know outside
there is a star
shining. My gratitude
so immense, my eyes
open and see black
is only a tone
generalising night,
darkness confessing
prayer after prayer.

Six. Clouds

A corridor of wind
blows unbeknownst
left to right of my
windows as though
a howling of intent,
direction. Only last night
we had spoken of the spiritual
as being that which
conversation leads through
the course of asking &
receiving. . .There are
still questions which come
again at night when moon
rises and eventuations –
such as a neighbours
white kitten entering your flat
via the balcony unexpectedly –
change your thoughts. . .

But these are the most beautiful.

The clouds today bringing a
little rain, which, puddling,
beckons such happily.

The Watch

A small child, he rests his elbow
on the window ledge and holds
his head in the palm of his hand.

Seated at the front of the car
a passenger or sidekick, he gazes
at the world outside the frame of
a window, just gentle skies and a
mild sun but the worry of something
much weightier in the fair-haired
boys splayed hand. Day almost whispering,
stay. Don't go anywhere beyond there

and return to think of fields;
and running until your palms rise.

For a Short Time, Liberty

Here, with each person's
attention engaged in the
private world of a
computer screen's wider
world, there is a
strange peace given by
the rule of silence
governing the library. People

speak, beside me, a couple

working collaboratively, speak
but their voices are hushed.

There is a peace settling
like wings. Here, the flight
settles, rests in the milieu
of interior worlds we immerse
ourselves in with thought.

Outside the wall of window

behind our long narrow bench
of blonde timber, outside
the opaque tint that subdues
light, the blades of a garden

shrub sway in mild winds.
Instead of distracting, it resonates
with our activity. It is an

emblem of a faraway place.

There is nothing else
but a clouded sky
behind it, a silhouette
of fuller dimensions.

No one wants to know

what the other is finding
in their world, we are,

in this, so very different
to our backdrop.

In the hours which passed
it has grown colder, just
as outside the trees are
more and more
bleak in their poverty.

In this coldness I start
to dream and again it exists
just as sometimes piano music

starts to play before it's
instrument is seen. A
musician's practice—it is the same.

Domesticity

Toward the end of March

a slowness took to its
last days. You could watch

ahead or count out a
remainder but even this
had, in mood of its expression,

a timelessness. Landscapes

were stretches of meadow
and wood whilst storms across

halted the gypsy heart: called it

to feel the colours of silvers, blacks,
greys: green of leaf, yellow autumn
flower and their sounds of poignant

character. Even in sleep then,
the sense of dreams was elevated
to stay, not go, in the illumined

mind, listening to this newly
ecstatic and talkative core.

The Broken Notes of Darkness

There was an interlude
preliminary to morning light
which contained only

an orchestra of crickets
amongst an audience of
wet leaves, serene after
rain and wanting of such –

music that speaks of augmenting.

In contrast, there was
a busyness in the afternoon streets
which told stories of people's
lives you could not ever
fully understand excepting
your own. Myself? I was

preoccupied by lamps as
a philosophical dialogue
between the quietude of
finishing a day's task,

for instance; and the warmth
such a thing could offer. Glancing
away, looking up or down

and sidelong, reflected
upon a wall, a lamp was
everybody's companion. It was

as though, after first contemplating

the idea of lamps from something
I had read, I saw their variety
more often, even, recently,

an Eastern one, handmade
out of fragments of red glass.

It has enriched my eyes

as a flood of gentle light
into a room can seem coming
from an outstretched hand.

A Ghosting

My washing billows
fabrics from an open-
necked, plastic Ikea bag
whose cloth handles
droop in dramatic, sweet
rest. Refinding it at
the front entrance to
home, I am a slave
to my own duties, gracious,
lifting it to hold it before
me royally, feeling its
weight like an old
burden, shuffling backwards
along the corridor
in socks without shoes.

Streetside Rose

To the winter sky
I couldn't have worn
the gloves they recommended
and caught the cockatoo.

To cold light, it was
too big for me, my hands.

To wind, a cardboard box
to take it to refuge was
still beautiful to the mind's
eye. To the song of rain

it no longer cries from
the lower branches
of the dark tree. To the
deep green leaves, it is
in the mirror mood
the lower side of a lake,
and lightly buoyant

To all the worlds cities
I feel he is in this light.

Coming

A seagull at the blue water's edge
collapses flight into nesting mode
and stares softly outwards
from a boardwalk's hewn verge.
Feathers lifted and folded
by a stable morning wind.

Weeks pass and I see a man
trying to say farewell
by walking in winter shoes
and clothes the downhill
of a beach embankment,
negotiating the moist, heavy
sand a fair portion of the
shoreline. His thirtyish
hands half in each of his
trousers side pockets, a gaze
that wants to look forward
but confessionally looks down
regularly: and this way speaks.

It is the same climbing down
a mountain, keeping
the summit's revelatory light
and true, utmost perfection

as if a dream you own
like an airy, soft cloud.

If there was faint music
heard by the seagull,
the man committed to
a voiceless parting
of ways, the journeyer
trekking their way
toward home it would

be this singing I hear
from females with high voices
whose chant is from another land
as vast as the whole of earth
but invariable in offering peace.

Before and Afterwards

The monotony of the waves breaking
near the shoreline was almost overpowering
in a synergy felt between the musical lulling
of their thunderous homecoming and another
summer's day of extreme heat—the haze shimmering
just above the water's surface, this, bejewelled sand.

A seagull in line with my gaze toward a sure
horizon opened its beak and craned its neck
as though to empty itself of the dryness or
perhaps, declare it an unshakeable truth;
and again, the waves thundered inwards,
white, molecular and relieved of significant
weights, a constant breeze meeting us, the bird.

You and I. Somewhere above all, in the deeper blue
of sky, the night before: the quietly burning stars
shining down and narratives of sleepers lifted
up, also now weightless. So that, these afternoon
hours lulled by the sea fulfil that which is empty;
and we carry it until the evening takes it, again.

Circus Act

A man, nondescript, unknown;
but laughing at a private joke,
called me over to his car to see.
"Come," he said, "You have to
see this". . .I dragged my feet over,
not wanting and not knowing
either, how to escape the fact
I'd inadvertently shared the joke.
"Mum," he said, "tried to fix
a scratch with some spray paint" –
I looked, almost one eyed I was
that reluctant. The car was white,
mum's artwork grey. I laughed
spontaneously: "Mum's a graffiti
artist!," I enthused. He laughed back,
"Well, an artiste anyway." I made
a noise, halfway between a polite
comic retort and a confusion
of thoughts. Why's that, I wanted
to say, but was already at my car.
Why did he take the graffiti out
of his mum's scrawl? Driving home
I thought about it, and looking up
the dictionary it was still
on my mind. I closed the book
sighing. Of all the small things.

Visiting the Archives at Six Ante Meridian

I was seventeen years old,
reading from hand-made
cue cards trimmed to size
with the household scissors.

On each, a detailed reference
of artworks written in blue biro
I would be examined on: name
of artist, title of work, date
and place of composition.

Reciting them, over and over
and turning page after page
of the History of Art to guess
a work, know them, by heart.

John Constable, The Mill,
Jules Bastien-Lepage,
The Potato Gatherers,
Camille Pissarro, Boulevard
Montmartre and so forth.

This morning I needed no
cue card to mouth slowly
Claude Monet, Rouen Cathedral
as the television news shared

footage of a church inferno,
the façade as gothic as the one
Monet watched sunlight blaze
in Normandy, soft in adoration.

The camera panned across
a bleak façade stiffly concrete
in fronting the intricacies
of exterior timber scaffolding,
the churches body, blackened
by fire, the cathedral floor
a bed of ruin, the black petals
of new ash scattering about
hopelessly in the silent air.

I held my coffee cup with
both hands, looking into its
centre where hot milk and
coffee blended in a swirl,
eddying to the polished,
caramel edges of its lacquered
interior, the outer ceramic
lending warmth, a matt white.

I drank from it, listening to
the sirens of fire trucks on
television and commentaries
about people weeping on

the streets of Paris. Later that
morning I visited the archives
of Monet's paintings, seeing
them recede and come forward
with "morning effect," "full
sunlight" or a "setting sun."

Gothic and eternally captured.

Though history had visited
Rouen too, to report damage
by lightning and hurricanes;
and after Monet, to report
stories of tall, falling towers,
melting bells after bomb raids
and shattered rose windows.

In Paris there is talk of rebuilding.
In Normandy, the cathedral
post renovation is growing old.
Tetelestai, archízei kai páli.

The Soul of a Sparrow

Here, in the reflected image,
all things brown are golden,
plain beige an exquisite ivory
cream; and twiglike,
fashioned, polished ebony.

The house sparrow's small head
drooped in late fatigue this
summer's day, bears her soul
in the bird bath's water –
the colour of brown garnet;

and daylight shimmers in the
body of it, her mirrored stance
there, not an occasion of
ruffled feather and sweaty,
flattened patches of down
but more immaculate grace.

Her feathers smooth, her large eyes
deeply the colour of night sky:
with moon seen and stars known
and all things heavenly, serenely
present. Eternal. Ah, love,

says the sparrow's soul and
the sun sparks white fireworks
into the haze of January heat.

And the bird drinks from it's
feeder, wets its feathered self
with the ponderance of it, smiling
what, in the image, could only be
the most beautiful smile imaginable.

The Crowd

People moved as though there was
a greater strength in standing tall

and the wind, the wind also moved

but not always with each one
person. At times you could believe
it deeply, smartly, in love

though never cease walking
so that it then humours, brings colour

to the colourless turmoil of
truth. No one looked for rain
in the sun's presence. No one

looked. The destination was inside
us and our legs orchestrated
the compulsion. Anyplace –

we were here. Could we predict
the moon ever? A full yellow

moon aligned perfectly
by a northwest star?

Only by not looking out.

Abiding and Else, Cat.

somewhere now. Didn't expect to see red Banksia
flowering from a low branch over the balcony. Never
once here, expected these rooms. Rain falling nightly,
sometimes daylong, mostly one whole sky in silver
with lucent clambers of nimbus. Across paths, overtly
heeded, yellow leaves; and cross-country the tree-roots
gnarled, decide bounding one foot at a time. Seeing someone
for an hour these low-rise buildings, no storey beyond five,
and a weaving of multifarious directions. One, yes, beautiful
oak, lowly circles of light amidst the shadows on a vast lawn.
That night earth's infinitesimal movement carries. An afternoon
sky in pale blue, some wispy idea of stratum. After storm and
pollen, storm and pollen, the days, the eyes flutter yet the
heart joyful. It's black and pumpkin thinking, Halloween,
some wild, crazy shadow across the moon, a discerned
shriek or no matter. Of both, there is this dusk retreating,
I, blinds drawn in the somewhere now. Candle bright table

Pink carnations in a vase, flowers furled, paper-thin
of petal. Somewhere the morning bird with eyes shut
to tonight's navy dark expanse, no stars, moon, never
sighted, the bedroom ghost bird, the Edward bird,
daylight's messenger. If the end of the week was fireworks,
tonight is early, the clank of crockery, phones ringing to
renditions of old phones ringing, the sound of prolonged
waiting on the line, the gaps between the trills. Someone

holding on somewhere, someone else trying to reach it
in time, that sense of clamouring, brilliance. The after-
dayness under a lamp. Blue sky morning, sunlight sparking,
a caterpillar slumps across my path, almost forever, almost
there. Every summit reached the sunlight seems the greater,
more a sense of Christ then; fallen twigs heaping, beige,
slender, debarked of varied length and kink. In the wind
fragrances belonging to memories best, human intimacies
that taste like, smell like, the inexpressible gravity. Apples!

At the beach comes the rain lightly, sunlight long retreated
over a distant edge, a sky of effusive grey clouds. Waves
sounding out endings at a shoreline, repetitive and musical,
as a loved one's sighing whilst sleeping. Whereas madly,
thunder & lightning is more an ear upon their chest or this
in reverse. In church that night, a child cries the soft whimpers
of panic in realising his attempt at climbing through a pew
has left him with his head one side and the rest of his good self,
another. Once freed, I turn away satisfied he looks like his father.
Deeply, the day settles to darkness, pitched and we scatter- run
with ambitious leaps, nimble as Eden folk. A night for the love of
two glazed cherries on a wooden pick. Not flying out of weather
but merging into it as the best aviators. Know a sweet dream.
Waking to Edward chirping nonstop into early light. Diffuse
sunburst across the black and white flowers of the eiderdown.
Five favourite books nestled spine outwards on a windowsill's
edge so they'll fade. Dear as moth's dust, insinuating wings.

Horses on courses for the two mile gallop, bets for name, rider
and number. Taking away in eyes, Honeysuckle, absently.
Interstate, the haze of sky almost rains then quietens to
invisible heat. A friend talks of Taree instead, of a lake, an
exotic population and a daughter whose new braces mean
she can't eat the Halloween lollies. Wanting to book the flight
home for Christmas but musing with the idea of driving,
that way a real sense of arriving. I'm torn between both,
taking sprints up the clay path from beach to concrete,
the brightness like that cliffside balcony where the wind
would blow fiercely and amplify the sound of the ocean.
I could sketch the clouds for how they resemble the love
inside ourselves. Effulgence; or as you put more delicately,
the many vicissitudes that carry. A raindrop falling, hits
my arm, not the brown linen dress; and bursts open. Like
at the restaurant that night when you kept standing to let
people in through the glass door, unceasingly, your height.

The Beauty of a Front Door

Is glass with dense opacity
and a patterning memorised
from hours watching the sea
move inwards, lapping and leave
in the same gesture. Is dark
wood with polish that frames
with great strength and divides
panes of this glass twice over
with cut strips of itself vertically
arranged. Is the feeling of turning
a key in the aged brass latch, hearing
the physicality of its heavy click
and pushing into the void of
hallway, palm to the timber of
the doors edge. Is nearly falling into
a space filled with light, a room
some distance with windows
this moment's witness. Is looking up,
standing in and closing the door
behind me, hearing it shut like
a lock. Is the world outside it
made into shapes and shadows
so as inside dreams have transport.

Rosh Hashanah

Waking to doves
singing ceiling to flight
with wordless tunes,
the world had come.

It had opened up.

White broderie pillowcases
and hard, irregular
portions of dark chocolate.

No one thing could be
said to be exactly lost.

Different stars for every night's
different heavens. Moonglow
reaching from highpoint to
stray dog's tear, chin mushed
upon paw. Last night in a morning.

Yellow sidewalk flowers
with shiny, black epicentres
replete with rain. They

sing of it, so overwhelmed
by their eaves it seems
home made it inevitable.

I drew a yawn, stretched
out my arms through air
and thought, I had not
been waiting. No, sunset,

last night, rouged its sky.

Postscript

Madrigal (of a 3D Star)

Then comes the hour of sunset.

In the darkening of trees,
there is a rising where there is
a falling. All passing traffic flows
like a deep river sloshing at the interpass
of opposing directions, slowing
and quieting in its drift toward
closure. From the middle room
of my interior, a dishwasher also
changes mechanisms to become
less rigorous and more subdued.

The trees, in their darkening, seeming
to grow taller and more voluminous
though the exaggeration is not toward
density. Instead, night is a complete picture.

There are high times of cerise pink
shot across the black-blue of sky
like descending comets. I am watching,
drifting outdoors with day and carried
back in by night's solace. The couch
and the wall, my legs folded under my body,
mingling puppet-like with shadows.
My room, uncomplicated by light.

Through the Looking Glass

Above her daughter by a bodies length,
she stands with her husband
at the edge of their balcony.

Their togetherness and bent stance
over the balustraded viewing platform
Shakespearian and impassioned.

The daughter gazes upwards,
her own love, her husband,
a little taller but so closely near
there is no space between their
inner sides. One moment, one time.

Quietly, the foursome converse
with private endeavour,
a cascade of red petalled
ivy pillaring the left side
of the upper-storey husband.

I am the bystander unnoticed,
completing my climb up a
steep suburban hill. I am a
chance witness to the beautiful.

At my back, downhill and past
the flat expanse of deep blue
ocean waters there is a city
so ghosted by rain and mist
it shows us no fire or complaint.

Flock

Cliffside, there are signs

areas beyond the boardwalk
are unstable and a danger to
life. Yet a couple recline

Manet style on a rock ledge
past the fence line and watch
the ocean without fear or shouts
of defiance. Nearing dusk,

light hits the rock and lends
it solidity so that, for a moment,
there is apparent asylum
in shadows. Past the narrow

trail to a long descent of stairs,
a solo traveller sits stubbornly top left
and pushes buttons on her mobile phone.

The view of the ocean tufted
white by autumn winds is immense
and travels all points of the compass.

Beyond every set of angular stairs
a long passage of slatted timber,
weary of salt, sunlight and storm.

Whole families amble their way upward
as though a chain of daisies flexible
only to the warp and dint of human traffic.

Instead of breaking it, I turn and walk back
the way I came, taking in with my senses

a late idea of emerald and dew, the girl
perched with her phone, the shadow
on the rock defending lovers and the

early fragrant night calling Monday
with the silky, steady voice of a cloud.

Open Windows

Day and the risen sun was bright.

A black wagtail rockets past me
clean on the horizontal plane
above eye level. A child clunks
his foot bike one eighty degrees to reroute
and race me, handicapped, to the trees.

Clouds heavy with moods find their rebirth
in smaller, smarter drifts of dreamscapes.

The sky, this way, becoming more and more
clear. Above kerbs, a see through, green, plastic
streamer flapping easily from a telegraph wire,
neither caught gallivanting or mournfully lost.

Premier

I want, for this room,
the sharp, sudden song of bellbirds
such that I heard this morning
from their high tree. Not to bring

inside an ecological calamity
but to lend the space a sharpness
of tone. True, to the naked ear,

the shrillness, the surprise of
a bellbirds call enraptures, speaks
of a future hour unseen, invisible,
inestimable and unexpected.

I want, for this room,
that alarming, arresting song.

Not to bring with it a prophecy
of the tragic but for it to awaken
me each time I enter the space
and thereby bring me in from
where I had been before. If

the song were there, coming

in through the windows
as though from earth's ceiling

I would look up before I look
down as a form of ritual. The

old parched palm branch on
the dark timber shelf of my bookshelf,
fronds either side of its spine
raised, more so with time, like wings,

would be delineated in the rectangular,
frameless mirror that sits at a
diagonal behind it. And delineated

twice over in its true form before
the mirror, by this new tone of
perfect notes. And that I do not

remember the Sunday it was
brought home from the church
would be a necessary thing, a
tool for the mind to know the
reality of replication. I want,

for this room, the high
call of bellbirds to bring in

the brightest notes of ether

so that my books are my
books, this lamplight that

hovers over my work is
a meditation on warmth,

the floorboards that stretch out
and display daylight have
no finitude to their shine.

I want, for this room, the cry
of bellbirds to signal everything
beyond its walls, windows and
doors is unseen, invisible,
inestimable and unexpected.

On the Impeccably Dressed

A white pigeon,
speckled with ink black
spots, walks back and
forth of a concrete
driveway. Large and
adult, the movement is
hardly easy as the pavement
is sloped. And although his
weight is not remarkable
the walking is slow,
seemingly studied. He has

a beautiful face.

It is very small, white and
round except pointed
in expression, due to
a short, black beak. Atop
a slender neck, it is a
serious, quiet face,
with black eyes that stare out
oblivious to my presence.

It is a warm afternoon but
the wind is gusty and occasionally
lifts the short feathers

of his body as though to
tease him out of his
reverie. It does not succeed.

The bird, above his chosen,
modernised surface of earth,
is at peace. I walk on
before he takes flight,
leaves for another patch of
land where he once more
might catch his breath,

enjoy the sun upon his
beautiful face. Therefore, it
makes sense to me that

later, in the middle of a
dark Autumn night, when
the wind is still robust,
undecided in the direction
of its currents and my
curtains conceal windows
that now feel cold and
moist with atmosphere,
that a person appears
to me in a dream. And
that person is a man wearing
a white jumper speckled with

ink black spots, some grey
shade of trousers and shoes,
shiny black with fresh rain.

It makes sense to me, in this
night of high winds and dim,
misted windows, that this
man appears in my dream
because this man is not
a stranger, but my father.

Oh God,

to wake to such knowledge.

Primary Colours

If love were a forward, spirited
tumble across new, damp grass
—of a distance, short and tight—
it would be here. There are

no gates at the entry. Instead, you

step in at whatever stride that days
energy carries, both real and
emotional by degrees. Stretching out

before you is a ribbon of a
cultured clay path, whilst
everywhere else is the same
new, damp grass that altogether

is the parkland reserve.
There are people everywhere.

Dispersed by family ties, friendship
or pet animal/ human relation

(even silver cats with delicate bells
march fondly behind their owners),

there are children with oversized bikes,

children wobbling vertically
on walking hands and dogs of
all sizes running circles without leads.

The sounds curve from high to low
across a stave of frequencies

appearing, hovering and disappearing

like ecstatic, sharp human voice calls

the dancing wind soon mutes.

Even in their segregated groups
these people stand with a devotion
not endorsed by a face toward a face

but a chaotic tenderness so free
that a back turned to contemplate
a view or supervise a child is
a pillar in the same temple.

I am here alone to be with you.

To look past the sharp sloping grassland
at the edge of the reserve. Miles away,

across the smooth grey patina of sea
is a city or irregularly tall buildings
and a reduced skyline. A single star

shines there, small, yellow and

bright. So that, in the stillness it

becomes interior: the other sky

it lights, familiarised by sweet

warmth. Night dark sky on earth,

here—If love were . . .

it is also a show of white flowers
on a branch of dark green leaves

falling arm's length over a fence line.

www.ingramcontent.com/pod-product-compliance
Lightning Source LLC
LaVergne TN
LVHW021552080426
835510LV00019B/2486